Round Up

A Texas Number Book

Written by Carol Crane and Illustrated by Alan Stacy

Sleeping Bear Press
310 North Main Street, Suite 300
Chelsea, MI 48118
www.sleepingbearpress.com

Sleeping Bear Press is an imprint of The Gale Group, Inc.,
a division of Thomson Learning, Inc.

Printed and bound in Canada.

10 9 8 7 6 5 4 3 2

Library of Congress Cataloging-in-Publication Data
Crane, Carol, 1933-
Round up : a Texas number book / by Carol Crane ; illustrated by Alan Stacy.
p. cm.
Summary: Various objects, animals, and people associated with the state of
Texas are presented in short rhymes, with added commentary, and used to
illustrate counting, multiplying, and adding.
ISBN 1-58536-133-X
1. Texas-Juvenile literature. 2. Counting-Juvenile literature. [1. Texas.
2. Counting. 3. Multiplication. 4. Addition.] I. Stacy, Alan, ill. II. Title.
F386.3 .C715 2003
976.4—dc21   2003010382

To William Anderson, author, educator,
and longtime friend.

CAROL

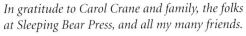

In gratitude to Carol Crane and family, the folks
at Sleeping Bear Press, and all my many friends.

For Mom and Dad in loving memory.

Deo Gratia.

ALAN

Rambling across Texas,
driving the mules through every turn.
As the chuck wagon hits the trail,
let's see what numbers we can learn.

So as we round up the herd,
come along for the ride.
In counting and history,
let us be your Texas guide.

1 chuck wagon
with wooden spoked wheels.
"Cookie" is very busy
preparing cowboy meals.

The chuck wagon is the cowboy's kitchen during a cattle roundup. Charles Goodnight, a Texas rancher, invented the chuck wagon in 1866. He and his partner Oliver Loving were taking a herd of 2,000 longhorn cattle on a major cattle drive. They needed a wagon big and strong that could carry food, water barrels, bedrolls, slickers for rain, a shovel, ax, branding irons, and pots and pans for at least 10 men. They decided the rear of the wagon should have a hinged lid that could be brought down and used for a worktable. It was like our kitchen counter today, where cutting, chopping, and mixing could be done. Mules pulled this heavy wagon.

The cook was called "Cookie." His work was never done. He had to gather the wood for cooking, make sure there were three big meals every day, and do this work in all kinds of weather. In the evening, it was his job to find the North Star. The wagon had to be headed toward the North Star so the cattle drive would know which way to head out in the morning.

one

1

The boot was designed to be a tool of the cowboy. High-heeled boots help to keep a cowboy's feet in the stirrups when he's riding his horse. The narrow toes are pointed so the cowboy can slide the boot easily into the stirrup. Spurs are metal wheels attached to the heels of the boot to touch the flank of the horse to spur him on, or make him go. The jingle of spurs is called "saddle music."

Today, men, women, and children go to the bootmaker to find just the right size boot. Have you ever stood on a paper, drawn around your foot and then measured to see how many inches long your foot is?

two

2

A pair of cowboy boots is our 2,
the very popular western shoe.
For walking, dancing, and riding broncs,
the bootmaker makes them just for you.

Does this sound like the story of the three little pigs? The javelina looks like a pig but is really a relative of the South American tapir, whose closest relatives are the horse and the rhino! The javelina lives in the Big Bend area of Texas. This animal will eat almost anything. Its most favorite food is the prickly pear cactus. Maybe that's why it is such a tough little animal. It lives in small family groups and does not like dogs.

The wolf is a large dog-like animal that can weigh 130 pounds. Running at speeds of 22 to 28 miles an hour for the first two miles, it can usually outrun its prey. In Texas, the wolf is on the endangered list.

three

3

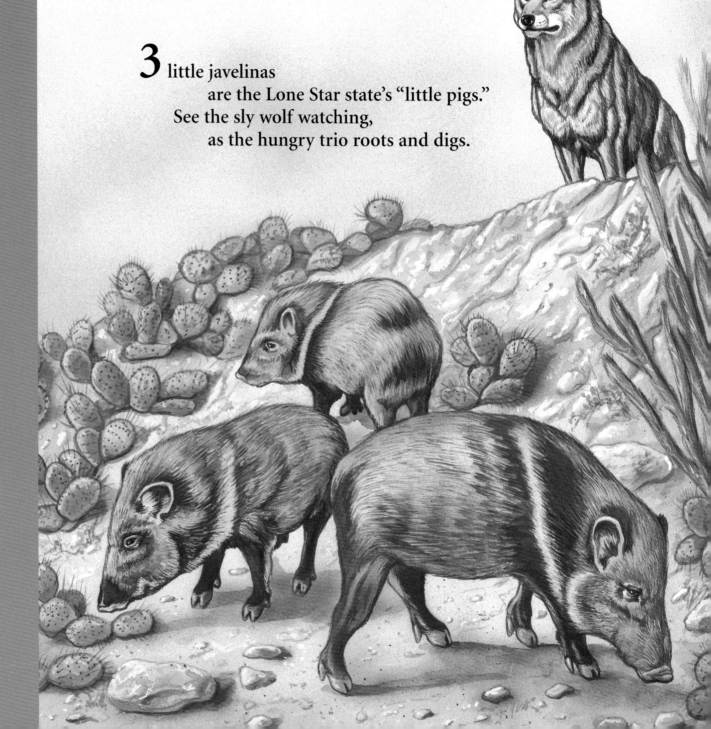

3 little javelinas
            are the Lone Star state's "little pigs."
See the sly wolf watching,
            as the hungry trio roots and digs.

A cowboy never goes out the door without his hat. The hat protects his eyes and neck from the sun, and he can use it as a bowl to catch rainwater to wash in. A cowboy tips his fingers to his hat and greets neighbors and stranger alike with a friendly smile. Out on the trail, while line- or square-dancing, or even riding a bucking bronco, cowboys have a way of keeping their hat on their heads.

Years ago, cowboys made $1 a day working on a ranch and would pay $10 to $20 for a good hat. How many days would he have to work before he could buy a hat?

Hats come in all sizes. In 1870 John B. Stetson made a hat that today is the most popular to wear, called a Stetson. Movie stars in westerns wore large hats called "10-gallon" hats during the 1930s, '40s, and '50s. Cowboys from Mexico are known for wearing the wide sombrero.

How are different hat sizes labeled? Have you ever measured your head for a hat?

four

4

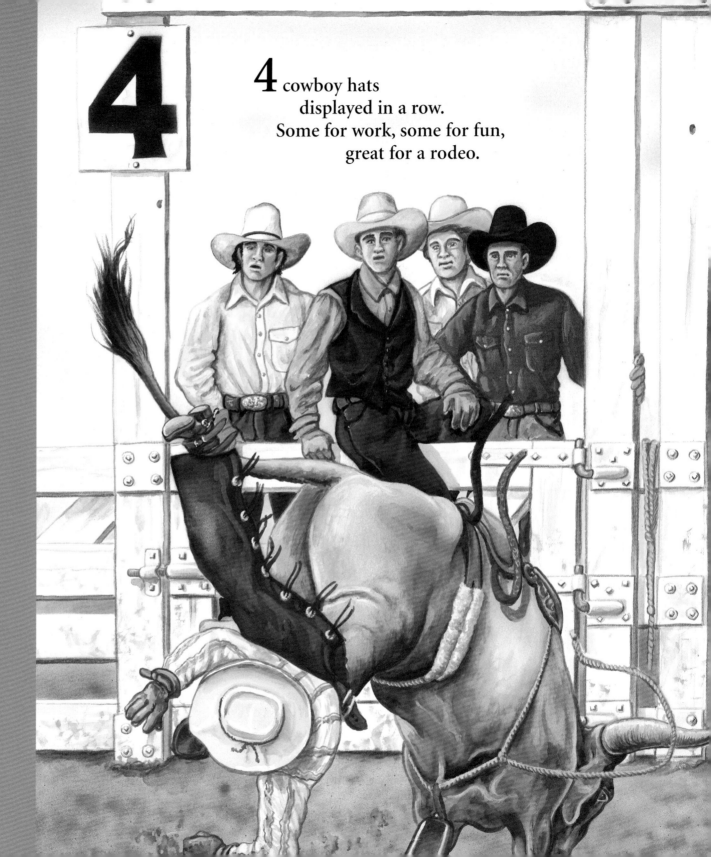

4 cowboy hats
displayed in a row.
Some for work, some for fun,
great for a rodeo.

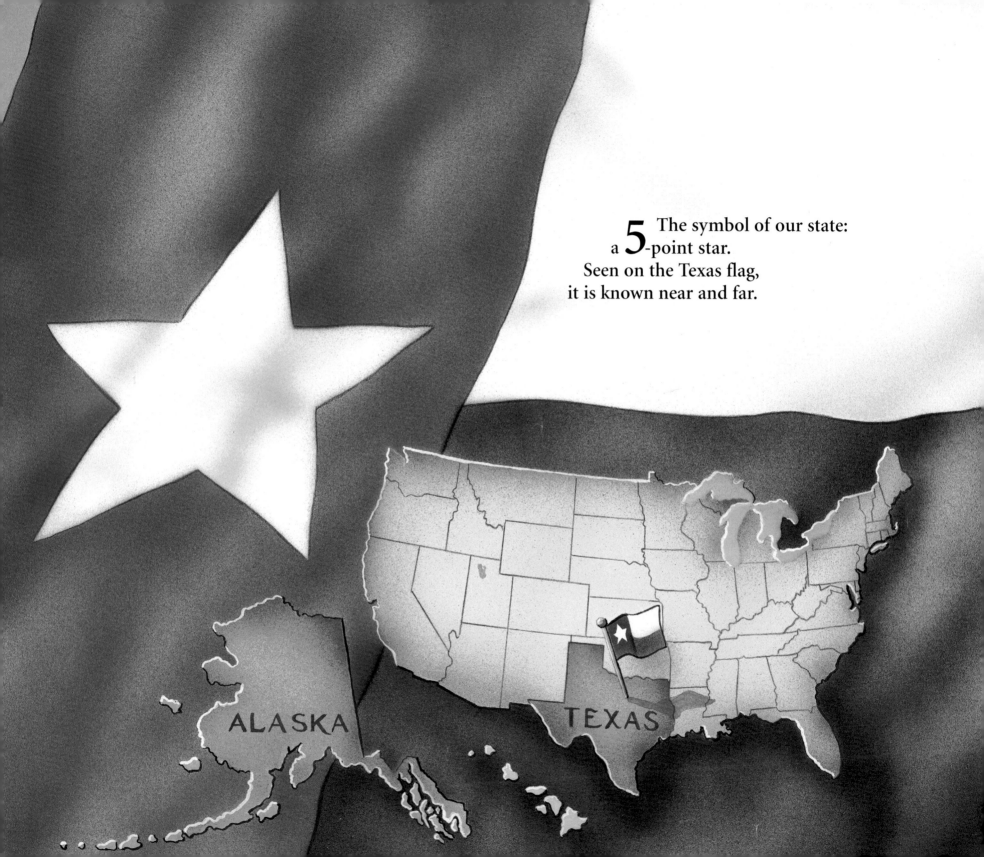

5 The symbol of our state:
a **5**-point star.
Seen on the Texas flag,
it is known near and far.

ALASKA

TEXAS

THE BETSY ROSS OF TEXAS

JOANNA TROUTMAN
1818 ~ 1879

LIBERTY or DEATH

Texas is the second largest state in our country. Texas' total size is as large as all of New England, New York, Pennsylvania, Ohio, and North Carolina combined.

In 1845 Texas became the 28th state to join the union. We needed a special flag to fly over this great state. The flag is a rectangle with a width-to-length ratio of two to three. It is divided into thirds:

1. A blue vertical stripe (up and down) the entire length of the flag along the left side = ⅓
2. Two equal horizontal stripes (across); one is white (⅓) and one is red (⅓).
3. A white five-pointed star is in the center of the blue stripe. One point faces upward.

A 17-year-old girl made the first "Lone Star" flag in 1835. Her name was Joanna Troutman and she was known as the "Betsy Ross of Texas." She designed the flag of white silk with a blue five-point star. Today in Austin stands a bronze statue of a girl standing and sewing.

five

5

Five hundred and fifty members of the Alabama Coushatta tribe live in the Big Thicket of East Texas. It is the oldest reservation in Texas. A large majority of the people speak their original, or native, language. The elders of the tribe teach language classes so that they may preserve their culture.

They also hold classes on weaving pine needle baskets. No two baskets are alike. Many are bowl-shaped, but some are animal-shaped. The first step in making the baskets is to collect and then dry the longleaf pine needles for two or more weeks. When the needles are dry they are woven into coils, and bound with the fibers from the raffia palm. Then when the weather is rainy or humid, the basket weavers start to make the baskets because the coils bend and are easier to work with. Small baskets take a few hours to make, but larger baskets can take weeks.

six

6

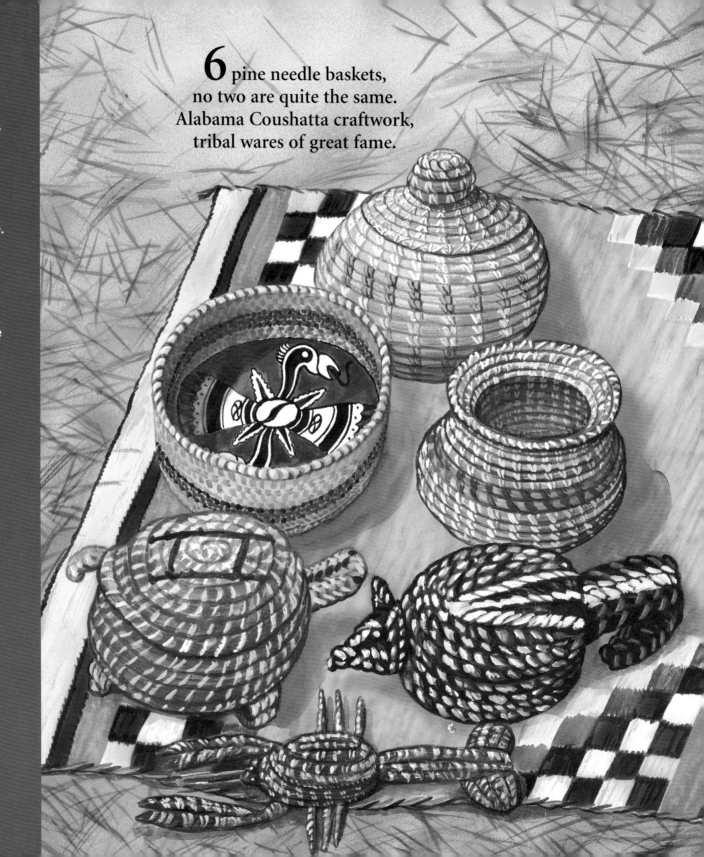

6 pine needle baskets,
no two are quite the same.
Alabama Coushatta craftwork,
tribal wares of great fame.

All but one of the state's 8,000-foot peaks are located in the Guadalupe Mountain range. Hunter Peak, Shumard Peak, Bush Mountain, Bartlett Peak, El Capitan, and Guadalupe Peak (which is the highest point in Texas at 8,749 feet) are all located there. In 1972 these mountains were established as the Guadalupe Mountains National Park.

Pioneers moving west and Native Americans used Guadalupe Peak as a landmark. Until 1880 the proud Apache nation used the Guadalupe Mountains as their last stronghold. In the early days of aviation, American Airlines erected a silver monument on the peak to help airplanes mark their routes. Coyote, mountain lion, mule deer, jackrabbits, and other wildlife use this mountain range as their home.

Mount Livermore, in Jeff Davis County, is the 7th mountain.

seven
7

Mountain peaks in Texas, is our number 7.
All higher than 8,000 feet, reaching up to heaven.

LUBBOCK
FORT WORTH • DALLAS
EL PASO
AUSTIN • HOUSTON
SAN ANTONIO

NEW MEXICO

CARLSBAD CAVERNS NATIONAL PARK

TEXAS

EL PASO
EL PASO CO.
HUDSPETH CO.
GUADALUPE MOUNTAINS NATIONAL PARK
REEVES CO.
WARD CO.
CULBERSON CO.
JEFF DAVIS CO.
8378' △ MOUNT LIVERMORE
PECOS CO.
PRESIDIO CO.
BREWSTER CO.
RIO GRANDE RIVER
BIG BEND NATIONAL PARK
MEXICO

GUADALUPE MTNS.
△
GUADALUPE PEAK
△
△
△
8749' △
EL CAPITAN 8085'
△
GUADALUPE MOUNTAINS NATIONAL PARK

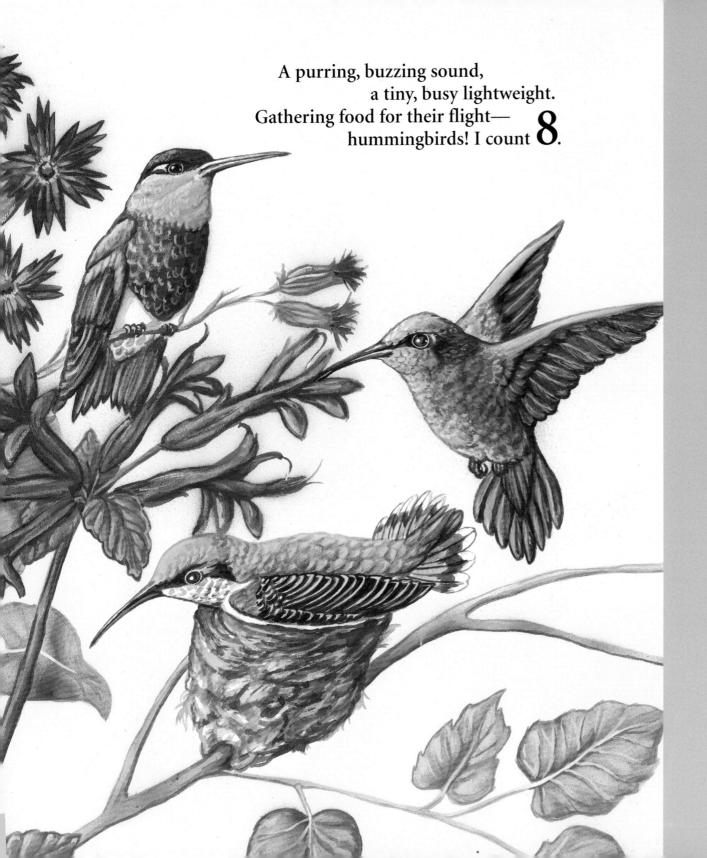

A purring, buzzing sound,
a tiny, busy lightweight.
Gathering food for their flight—
hummingbirds! I count **8**.

Hummingbirds migrate through Texas in large numbers in the fall and stay along the coast, eating and gaining weight before attempting to cross the Gulf of Mexico. They migrate to Mexico and Costa Rica for the winter.

There are at least 17 different species of hummingbirds that visit Texas. The smallest one is 2½ inches long. Hummingbirds are attracted to red, tubular flowers. They love the sugar in the flowers as well as the insects and spiders found there. They will also eat from feeders that are filled with sugar water. The ruby-throated hummingbird will defend its feeder or flowers from other hummingbirds.

Hummingbirds can hover in the same place while they eat, and are the only birds able to fly backward!

eight

8

Seeming to run through fountains, splashing water at the statues' feet, this sculpture shows the mustang as it once grazed and roamed the Texas plains. There is a lead stallion, followed by a young stallion, five mares, and two colts. The artist Robert Glen worked eight years to complete the statues.

The mustangs of Las Colinas are the world's largest sculptures. The bronze horses were made in England and each horse weighs approximately two tons. They were shipped to Texas on an airplane. They arrived at Dallas/Fort Worth Airport and then were taken to Irving, Texas, where each horse was placed on an 8,000-pound concrete base. The plaza honors the mustang with pride and remembrance.

nine
9

The **9** mustangs of Las Colinas—
sculptures larger than life.
Galloping across a stream of water—
free, spirited wildlife.

Now we see our number **10**—
Cadillac cars all in a row.
Buried with their noses down,
an artists' graffiti show.

Near Amarillo, Texas, you can find the landmark called "Cadillac Ranch." It is located off old Route 66. Many tourists stop by to take pictures of this display of cars, buried with their grills down and large dolphin tail fins pointing upward into the Texas sky. The original colors were sky blue, gold, banana yellow, and turquoise. Today, the cars have coats of graffiti and doodle art sprayed over them.

ten
10

Football is the number-one sport in Texas. If it is high school football, every parent and student cheers for his or her favorite team on Friday night. College football on Saturdays is always played to sellout crowds. Then, on Sunday, the professional teams play in stadiums, where the roar of the crowd is awesome. Football is the biggest game in town. Football in the Lone Star state is so powerful it has been declared "king of sports."

eleven
11

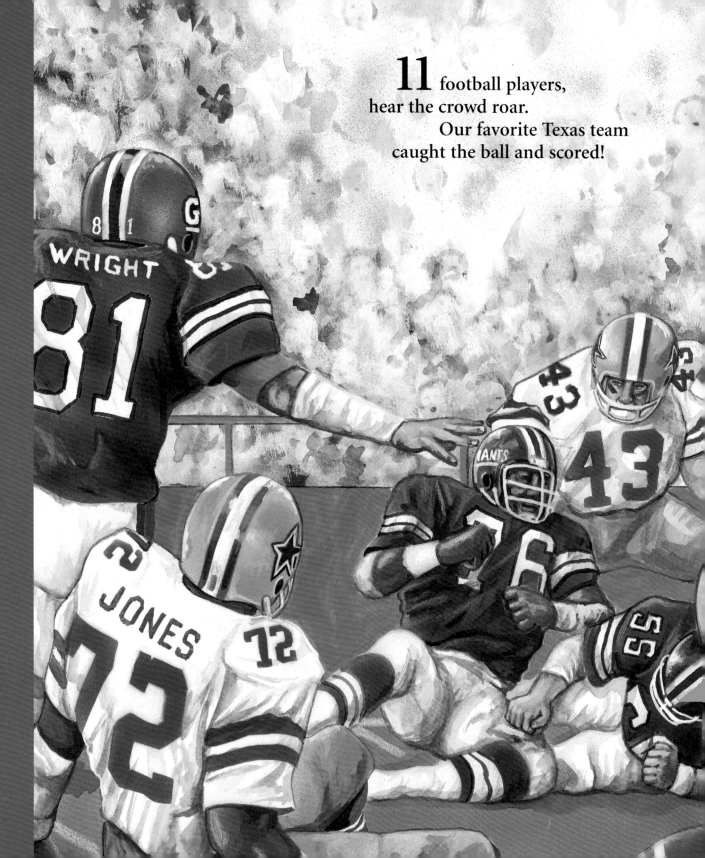

11 football players, hear the crowd roar. Our favorite Texas team caught the ball and scored!

The word "mariachi" is from the language of the Coca Indians. It means "musician," or any person engaged in making music. You can tell a mariachi group is playing by their style of music, dress, and instruments. The dress of the mariachi group is called a "traje." They wear a *sombrero* (broad-brimmed hat), a *mono* (large bow tie), a *chaleco* (short jacket), *botines* (or ankle boots), snug trousers without back pockets, a wide belt, and *botonaduras* (shiny buttons) on the side of the pants.

The instruments consist of one or two violins, the vihuela, guitars, trumpets, and a guitarron. The violinists play the melody and the trumpets add strength to the songs. You can also hear the "gritos," which are shouts and cries made during the music by the band.

Music is an important part of Mexican culture. Texas has many festivals where this music is heard and enjoyed. The festive mariachi melodies are played at weddings, anniversaries, birthdays, picnics, and barbecues.

twelve
12

Listen: do you hear that sound?
Music in the old tradition.
12 violins, guitars, and trumpets,
mariachi musicians.

Texas raises about 90% of the Angora goats in the United States. These little white goats originally came from Turkey. In 1849 seven does (females) and two bucks (males) were imported into this country. Now the United States has become one of the largest producers of the long, wavy, and shiny mohair. The mohair is sheared from the goats and woven into clothing and blankets. An adult goat will produce 8 to 16 pounds of mohair a year.

Goats are docile animals and can eat an assortment of tough weeds in a pasture. They like brush, tree leaves, and rough plants like Canada thistle, sandburs, or sagebrush.

thirteen
13

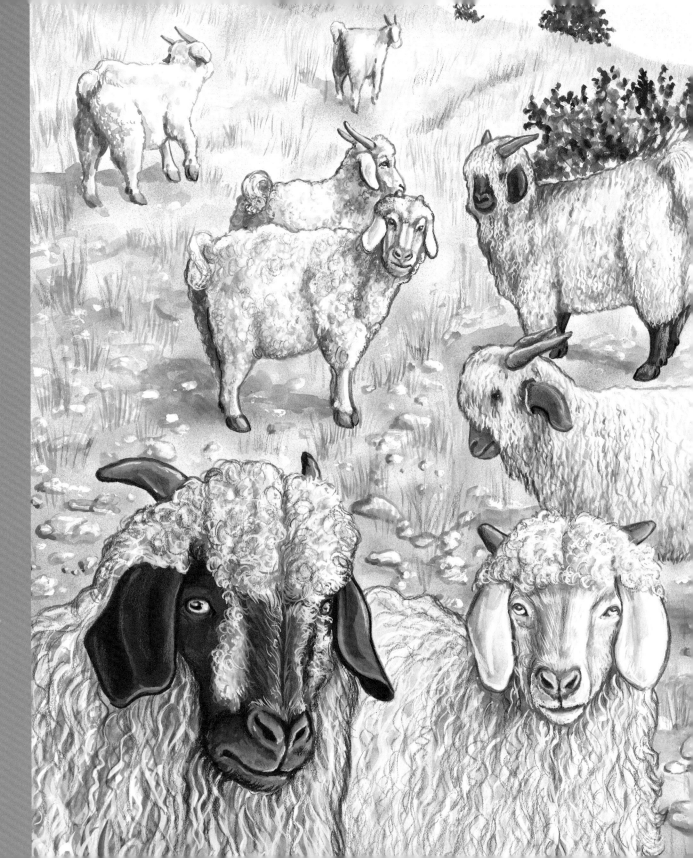

Soft and warm mohair
shorn from **13** Angora goats.
The spinners are making yarn
from white and glossy coats.

Over the years, wind, water, animals, insects, and birds have spread many different wildflower seeds throughout the state. This has resulted in a variety of colors in a beautiful floral display. Texas has many different climates, from very warm to bitter cold, and still these wild plants grow. Many school-children learn the importance of leaving wildflowers alone to help them multiply and thrive.

Sometimes, watching butterflies flit from flower to flower makes a remarkable show along a country road.

fourteen
14

14 various wildflowers
blending colors all together.
A Texas landscape painting,
in sunny or rainy weather.

Standing like soldiers on a dusty rural road, **15** mailboxes all sharing the same zip code.

254 SMITH
255 JONES
257 ORTIZ
259
U.S. MAIL 260

BENJAMIN FRANKLIN
1706~1790

CAMAS

YELLOW MEADOW BEAUTY

GOAT'S BEARD

CINQUEFOIL

UNICORN PLANT

BIRD'S-FOOT VIOLET

BUTTON BUSH

SILVER BELL

In 1775 Benjamin Franklin was named the first Postmaster General by the Continental Congress. The history of mail delivery from ship, pony express, railway, and by air would amaze this statesman!

In 1896 the first experimental rural delivery routes began. Texas did not have rural free delivery (RFD) until the 1900s. The postal carrier would deliver mail over rutted roads and through forests in all kinds of weather.

Texas families put mailboxes in one location that was a central distance between farms. The development of better roads and highways in America was a by-product of rural free delivery.

After much experimenting, on July 1, 1963 a five-digit code was given to addresses throughout the country. This system was called ZIP codes, for Zoning Improvement Plan. The first number is the geographical location in the United States. The number 7 means the location is Texas. Do you know your ZIP code?

fifteen
15

20 cowboy handkerchiefs—
large loose cloths of reds and blues.
Tied around the cowboy's neck,
set for dusty trail *ah-choos.*

Cowboys had many uses for the large pieces of cloth called handkerchiefs. They never went out on the range without one tied loosely around their neck. A handkerchief could be quickly pulled up over their face to keep dust or bugs out of their eyes, nose, or mouth.

Often the handkerchiefs were used to wrap up food so cowboys could eat out on the range as they were riding along. It could also be used for keeping the sun off their necks, slings for broken arms, or belts for tying small calves onto the saddle. The cowboy had many uses for this square of cloth.

How many different uses can you think of for handkerchiefs? How many shapes can you fold a square into?

twenty
20

With a good tailwind, the tumbleweed can move very fast across the prairie. The plant does not stay stuck in the soil. Once the seeds are ripe in the plant, it breaks away from the main stem. As the wind moves it over the land it deposits about 250,000 seeds that were stored inside. The tumbleweed looks like a big ball. When it hits the ground, because of its design, it will not lose all of its seeds in one bounce.

As the bush grows to almost three feet tall, it becomes sticky to the touch. The very sharp, pointy leaves will go through heavy leather gloves, and can easily cut a horse's legs.

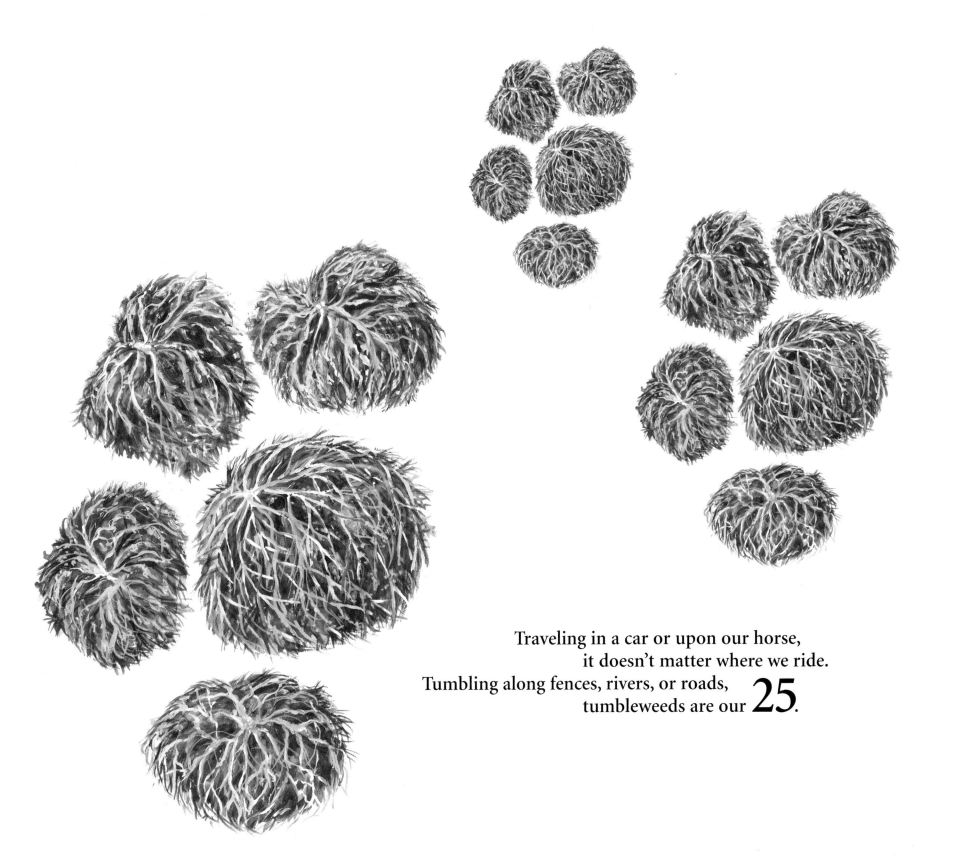

Traveling in a car or upon our horse,
it doesn't matter where we ride.
Tumbling along fences, rivers, or roads,
tumbleweeds are our 25.

Cornhusk dolls have been made for centuries, beginning with Indian mothers and pioneer women. The husks formed a dress and apron. A round pebble was wrapped in husks for the head. The corn tassels could be used for hair.

Corn or maize has been grown in Texas from prehistoric to present times. It has many uses. Texans used cobs for jug and bottle stoppers, tool handles, back-scratchers, torches, fishing floats, and firewood. The shucks from corn were used for writing paper and stuffed into mattresses and pillows. Also, the husks were used for wrapping foods such as tamales, ash cakes, and fruits.

Children used the kernels for markers in board games. Even the stalks and leaves had many uses. Pioneers used them for scarecrows, light fencing, and roof thatching. The corn was made into cornbread, mush, grits, fritters, and our favorite, popcorn! Corn is the basic ingredient in tortillas, tamales, *posole*, and *atole*. At harvesttime, families gathered for shucking frolics, or "bees."

30 cornhusk dolls
waiting for playmates.
Made at the county fair,
miniature lightweights.

40 baked peanut butter pies
cooling on the five shelves.
How many can you count,
starting with four to twelve?

Growing peanuts began in Texas about 1906. They were originally sold to a confectionery factory for peanut oil, peanut butter, and candy. By 1940 former cotton fields were planted with the Spanish peanut. The peanut plant needs a growing season of about five months without frost. It also needs moderate rainfall, lots of sunshine, and sandy soil.

It was discovered that the peanut vines make good livestock feed. In 1991 Texas was ranked as the second largest peanut-growing state in the nation. Have you ever shucked one full cup of peanuts to see how many peanuts that would be? A quarter of a cup? A half-cup? Or three-quarters of a cup?

forty

40

50 prairie dogs
living in prairie dog towns.
Jumping, scurrying around—
little brown circus clowns.

The prairie dog is a close cousin to the ground squirrel. In the 1900s there was a prairie dog "town" in the high plains of Texas that was 100 by 250 miles in size! An estimated 400 million prairie dogs lived in this "town." The prairie dog digs a burrow, which has tunnels and a narrow opening to protect his family from predators. When an enemy approaches he gives a bark to warn the colony and then plunges below.

A camera is a must when visiting a prairie dog town. They roll, tumble, kiss each other, and become very excited when anyone approaches their burrow.

fifty
50

On the trail, cowboys each have their own jobs to do. Some ride near the front of the herd, while others keep the cattle together with their lariats swinging from side to side. The cowboys talk to the cattle and coax them on. Other cowboys ride at the end of the herd and make sure there are no stragglers. It is a dusty job to ride at the back of the cattle herd.

Longhorn cattle have long legs, can go farther without water, and manage the long cattle drives better than other breeds. They often have horns that are five to six feet from tip to tip. Many times there were 1,000 to 4,000 longhorns in a cattle drive.

A young cowboy who is learning the ways of the trail is called a wrangler. He looks after the horses. He keeps them fed and watered. A cattle drive is hard on the horses, so cowboys change horses three times a day.

one
hundred
100

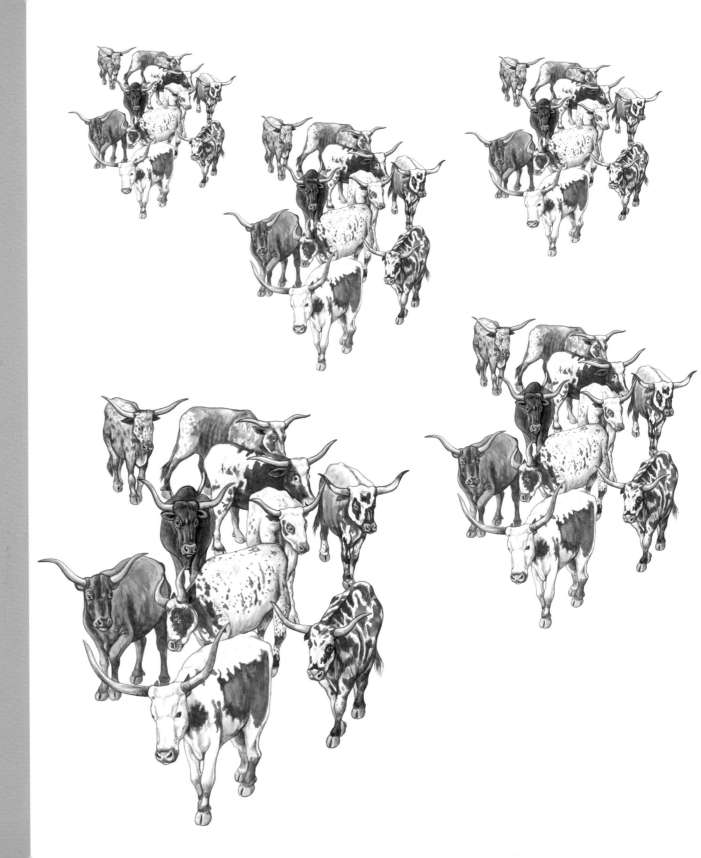

Get along little doggies,
the trail is coming to an end.
We've pushed **100** longhorn cattle;
Abilene is 'round the bend.

Carol Crane

Carol Crane is delighted to return to the Lone Star state—where she and her husband first traveled as newlyweds. She has also written *Sunny Numbers: A Florida Counting Book*, as well as alphabet books for Florida, Alaska, Georgia, South Carolina, North Carolina, and Alabama.

Carol is a respected national education consultant, known as a "walking, talking bibliography of great children's literature" by numerous teachers, librarians, and parents. She travels the country throughout the year talking about children's books at conferences and schools. When not on the road, she and her husband Conrad call Michigan and North Carolina home.

Alan Stacy

Alan drew his first painting at the age of 18 months—on a wall at home! Luckily, his mother—also an artist—encouraged him from the start, enrolling him in an adult drawing class at the age of eight. Alan's father, an Air Force pilot, took the family to Germany, Virginia, Alaska, and New Mexico before settling in Texas in 1975. Alan credits his family's travels for his profound love of animals and nature, which is reflected in his art.

Alan worked in broadcast television as a graphic artist for many years before becoming a self-employed illustrator and designer. Alan also teaches cartooning, comic book art, and illustration. He is also the illustrator for *L is for Lone Star: A Texas Alphabet*. He lives in Arlington, Texas.